Deeper Waters

21 Day Intimacy Challenge

ABI OYEBODE

ISBN (Paperback): 979-8-9931941-0-3
ISBN (eBook): 979-8-9931941-1-0

Published by Live Grow Thrive LLC
Columbia, MD

Cover design and interior layout by @charlyn_designs
Printed in the United States of America
First Edition

CONTENTS

Week 3: Go Deep

DEDICATION

To every heart that longs to know Him more—
this is for you.

To the weary worshipper, the hidden intercessor,
and the one who's been quietly crying out for more of God...
May these 21 days become the spark of a lifelong fire.

And above all,
To the One who first loved me —
this offering is for Your glory.

HOW TO USE THIS BOOK

Welcome to Deeper Waters: A 21-Day Intimacy Challenge!

Whether you are doing this as part of our **21-Day Intimacy Challenge Fast** or doing this devotional independently, this journey is designed to help you draw closer to God in a deeper, more personal way. Each day includes:

- **Teaching** – a short, powerful lesson rooted in Scripture
- **Reflection Questions** – prompts to help you go deeper
- **Prayer Focus** – specific prayer points to align your heart with His

We also encourage you to pair this devotional with the **Deeper Water: 21 Day Intimacy Challenge Companion Journal**. The journal offers:

- Daily space to write out your thoughts and prayers
- Additional **scriptures for meditation**
- **Thoughts for Today** – practical truths to reflect on
- A place to track what God is revealing, day by day
- Extended journaling space for reflection and breakthrough

Choose Your Pace:

- Follow the daily schedule one day at a time for 21 days.
- Or join us during our **live annual fast**, which includes prayer calls, group discussion, and live teaching for deeper accountability and support.

Tip: Keep your Bible, this devotional, and the companion journal handy! You will need them during this time of intimacy with God.

Whether you're reading on your own or journeying with our community, one thing is certain: *God longs for your heart. And He's ready to meet you—right where you are.*

WEEK 1

Draw Nearer

CHAPTER 1

A New Day

(WEEK 1 DAY 1)

A Call to Intimacy

Congratulations on beginning this 21-day intimacy challenge! Many start with good intentions but never take the steps to truly draw near to God. Yet you said yes and that yes matters, so congratulations! As you embark on this journey, I believe there will be a transformation in your relationship with the Father that will lead to tangible transformation in your life.

The truth is, you are responsible for your level of intimacy with the Father. We initiate the depths of the intimacy. But for many of us the pull of the world is stronger than our desire for God.

> *Come close to God, and God will come close to you.*
> *Wash your hands, you sinners; purify your hears, For*
> *your loyalty is divided between God and the world*
> — **James 4:8**

God has already extended His invitation. The cross was His outstretched hand, His unmistakable declaration: I willing lay down my life to purchase yours so you can come back to me. The question is no longer Does God want me? but How will I respond to His Invitation?

One of the greatest revelations you can ever receive is this: God desires you more than you desire Him. God is more passionate about being intimate with you than you are about Him. How do I know this? James 4:5 tells us:

> *Do you think the Scriptures have no meaning? They say that God is passionate that the spirit he has placed within us should be faithful to him*

That thought alone is staggering. The Creator of the universe thinks about you more than the grains of sand on the seashore. He longs for a closeness that exceeds every human relationship you've ever experienced.

> *How precious are your thoughts about me, O God. They cannot be numbered! I can't even count them; They outnumber the grains of sand! And when I wake up, you are still with me!* – **Psalm 139: 17-18**

When you think of intimacy with God, think beyond just prayer or reading your Bible. Think of Him as your daily companion, your best friend, your cheerleader, and your personal GPS navigation system. Just as hunger drives us to food and thirst drives us to water, cultivating intimacy with God will build up your spirit which will draw you into His Presence day after day. Drawing near requires intentionality it does not happen by accident.

- **Intentional Space**: Initially, prayer will not be instinctive. You will not naturally gravitate towards prayer. You must decide to set aside the time.
- **Intentional Focus**: You must remove all distractions. Jesus often withdrew to desolate places to pray (Luke 5:16)

- **Intentional Pursuit**: Just as relationships grow through pursuit, God invites you to seek Him with all your heart (Jeremiah 29:13).

God Wants All of You

Too often we offer God partial surrender. We give Him our Sunday mornings but not the rest of our week. We give Him empty words but not our hearts or our thoughts. We give Him the leftovers but not our first fruits. We offer Him songs but not our worship. Yet, intimacy with God demands all of you.

Romans 12:1 calls us to offer our bodies as a *living sacrifice, holy and pleasing to God this is your true and proper worship*. This means that every part of who you are belongs to Him.

- **Your Mind** – What you think about, imagine, or meditate upon should glorify Him (Philippians 4:8).
- **Your Heart** – Your desires, motives, and affections should be aligned with His will (Proverbs 4:23).
- **Your Body** – Even your physical choices how you steward your health, your purity, your actions reflect your devotion to Him (1 Corinthians 6:19-20).
- **Your Time** – How you spend your days reveals what you treasure most (Ephesians 5:15-16).

God wants your dreams, your fears, your relationships, your ambitions everything. The hidden corners where shame, pain, or disappointment reside? He wants those too.

Why? Because His glory dwells not only among us but within us.

> *The Word became flesh and made his dwelling among us. We have seen his glory, the glory of the*

> *one and only Son, who came from the Father, full of grace and truth* – **John 1:14 NIV**

> *For God wanted them to know that the riches and glory of Christ are for you Gentiles too. And this is the secret: Christ lives in you. This gives you assurance of sharing his glory* – **1 Colossians 1:27**

When you surrender all, His glory begins to flow freely through every area of your life, revealing His nature to those around you. Your life, family, career, business, education, and relationships become conduits for God to manifest His glory.

Think of it this way: when a lightbulb is connected to power, it cannot help but shine. But if part of the wiring is faulty or disconnected, the light flickers or fails to turn on. In the same way, areas of your life that are not surrendered can short-circuit the flow of His glory.

The Glory Within You

2 Corinthians 5:17 tells us if anyone is in Christ, he is a new creation; old things have passed away; behold, all things have become new. This means intimacy isn't just personal – it's transformative. When God has all of you, His nature becomes visible to others through your life.

- **Peace in Chaos** – Philippians 4:7 promises a peace that transcends understanding. People will see you display calmness in the midst of storms and challenges that would make others crumble. That is glory revealed.
- **Love in Opposition** Matthew 5:44 calls us to love even our enemies. When you respond with grace instead of anger and retaliation when mistreated, His glory is revealed.

- **Joy in Trials** James 1:2 reminds us to count it all joy in difficulty. When joy flows in difficult times, it testifies to a strength beyond human ability. That is glory revealed

Glory revealed is not always about miracles or dramatic signs. Often times, it is about consistency of character, perseverance, and the quiet strength of a surrendered life.

Think about how Moses face shone after being with God (Exodus 34:29 30). He didn't try to shine; the glory of God simply radiated from him because of time spent in intimacy. Likewise, when believers spend time in the secret place with God, His Presence is naturally revealed through them.

God's desire is not only to fill you with His presence but to reveal His presence through you. You are His temple and His Spirit dwells in you. (1 Corinthians 3:16). That means every encounter you have – whether at home, in the workplace, or in passing conversations – can become a holy encounter. An opportunity for others to encounter Him because His glory is flowing freely through you.

Reflection Questions

1. Does God truly have all of you? If not, what areas are you withholding?
2. Is His glory evident in every area of your life? If not, which areas need His touch?
3. What revelation do you need from the Holy Spirit to perceive His glory fully?

Prayer Focus

1. **Revelation**

   Lord, give me a clear revelation of my heart and life. Show me where I've fallen into the enemy s traps. Open my eyes to see what You see and open my heart to know what You know. Remove every barrier keeping me from going deeper with You.

2. **Repentance**

   Father, I come with a clean and contrite heart. Purge me of everything hindering intimacy with You. Create in me a clean heart and renew a steadfast spirit within me.

Key Takeaway: God is not hiding from you; He is waiting on you. The question is: Will you draw nearer?

CHAPTER 2

What do you hunger for?

The Power of Spiritual Hunger

Congratulations on choosing to show up again today! Every time you make space for God, you are declaring to Him that He matters more than your schedule, your comfort, and your convenience. The Lord recognizes and honors hunger for Him.

Hunger is powerful because it determines pursuit. If you are hungry for success, you will work tirelessly to achieve it. If you are hungry for approval, you will seek it out-even at the expense of your peace. The same is true spiritually: the depths you are willing to go in pursuit of God reveals the depths of your hunger for Him.

David expressed this in Psalm 63:1 (NKJV): *O God, You are my God; early will I seek You; My soul thirsts for You; My flesh longs for You in a dry and thirsty land where there is no water.* David's hunger was not passive; it was consuming. His longing for God shaped his daily priorities and caused him to seek God early, before anything else.

Spiritual hunger is not a casual interest. It is a driving force that pushes you beyond comfort and convenience. Just as physical hunger leads you to food, spiritual hunger compels you into prayer, worship, fasting, and the Word. When you are truly hungry for God, you will pursue Him in ways that go beyond your routine or comfort.

You Hunger for What You Feed On

The reality is this: *we are what we consume.* Spiritually, emotionally, and mentally, we are shaped by what we continually allow into our lives.

- Feed on the world, and your appetite will be for worldly things.
- Feed on God's Word, and your appetite will increase for Him.

Jesus said in Matthew 4:4 (NKJV), "*Man shall not live by bread alone, but by every word that proceeds from the mouth of God.*" Just as food sustains your physical body, God's Word sustains your spirit.

Paul reinforces this truth in Philippians 4:8 (NIV): "*Finally, brothers and sisters, whatever is true, whatever is noble, whatever is right, whatever is pure, whatever is lovely, whatever is admirable – if anything is excellent or praiseworthy – think about such things.*"

If you allow negativity, gossip, fear, or constant distractions to occupy your mind, they will quash your hunger for God. But when you continually fill your heart and mind with the things of God – the Word, prayer, worship – and engage in godly fellowship, your appetite for God increases.

Think of it like food: if you eat fast food every day, your body will crave sugar and grease. But if you regularly eat fresh fruits and vegetables, your body begins to crave what is healthy. In the same way, spiritually, your cravings are shaped by what you continually consume.

Making Room for God

Hunger is not just emotional – it is practical. We make time for what matters. Look at your calendar. What takes up the majority of your time and attention?

Jesus said in Matthew 5:6, *"Blessed are those who hunger and thirst for righteousness, for they shall be filled."* Hunger is shown by what you prioritize.

- If you are hungry for God, you will wake up earlier to pray.
- If you are hungry for God, you will fast to quiet the voice of your flesh and sharpen the voice of the Spirit.
- If you are hungry for God, you will cut back on entertainment or social media to make room for the Word.

Spiritual hunger is expressed through action. True hunger will reorder your life around God's Presence.

When your soul hungers for God, you will create space to pursue Him. And as you do, He promises to fill you!

Reflection Questions

1. Is your soul hungry for God or are you seeking His hand more than His heart?
2. What are you feeding your soul daily—the Word of God or worldly noise?
3. What practical steps can you take to develop spiritual hunger like David in Psalm 63?

Prayer Focus

1. **Hunger**

   Father, reset my appetite for You during this fast. Renew my hunger for Your presence and Your Word. Replace every unhealthy craving with a longing for You alone.

2. **Intentionality**

   Lord, help me to be intentional about what I watch, listen to, and think on. Teach me to feed my spirit with truth and life-giving things. Let my thoughts align with Philippians 4:8 so that what I meditate on builds hunger for You

Key Takeaway: You hunger for what you feed on. Feed on the Word of God, His presence, and His truth—and your soul will crave Him more.

CHAPTER 3

Obedience and Holiness

(WEEK 1 - DAY 3)

The Call to Obedience

If you are reading this today, congratulations – you haven't given up on the challenge! That persistence matters because intimacy with God is forged in moments when you feel like stopping but choose to press on.

Obedience is a key marker of intimacy. Scripture teaches us that intimacy with God requires humility, and humility leads to obedience. When God gives an instruction, our response reveals the true posture of our hearts.

Samuel confronted Saul with this sobering truth:

> *"What is more pleasing to the Lord: your burnt offerings and sacrifices or your obedience to His voice? Listen! Obedience is better than sacrifice, and submission is better than offering the fat of rams"* –
> **1 Samuel 15:22**

Obedience is not about religious activity or outward performance. God is not impressed by empty rituals or superficial devotion. What He desires is a heart fully yielded to His voice.

True obedience says, "*Yes, Lord*," before the details are even revealed. It trusts His wisdom more than our reasoning, His timing more than our preferences, and His ways more than our comfort.

Obedience Is Doing

Obedience is not passive. It's not a feeling—it's an action. It requires movement. James reminds us that "*faith by itself, if it is not accompanied by action, is dead*" – James 2:17 NIV

- *Immediate obedience matters.* Delayed obedience is often another form of disobedience.
- *Partial obedience is still disobedience.* King Saul learned this when he spared what God told him to destroy (1 Samuel 15). God is not looking for selective submission; He wants complete obedience.
- *Costly obedience refines faith.* Sometimes obedience will require you to lay down comfort, reputation, or convenience. Abraham's willingness to sacrifice Isaac was not about ritual – it was about demonstrating complete trust in God (Genesis 22).

Obedience is radical: when God speaks, we act even when our flesh resists, even when others don't understand, and even when it doesn't make logical sense.

Think of Noah. Building an ark when there was no rain on the earth seemed foolish, yet his obedience preserved his family and fulfilled God's plan. Radical obedience positions you for supernatural breakthrough.

Holiness Flows From Obedience

Holiness is not merely avoiding sin; it is being set apart and fully yielded to God so that His character flows through your life. Holiness is not about perfection but about alignment, bringing every thought, word, and action into agreement with His nature.

Peter reminds us:

> *But just as He who called you is holy, so be holy in all you do; for it is written: 'Be holy, because I am holy* – **1 Peter 1:1516 NIV**

Holiness is the fruit of obedience. When you consistently obey, your life begins to take on the likeness of Christ. Over time:

- Your speech becomes more gracious.
- Your thought life grows purer.
- Your responses reflect patience, kindness, and self-control.
- Your desires shift from self-centered to God-centered.

Holiness becomes less about striving and more about reflecting the One you are walking with. It is not achieved by your own effort but birthed from intimacy with God.

Jesus said, *"If you love me, keep my commands"* (John 14:15 NIV). Love expressed through obedience is the pathway to holiness. When obedience becomes your lifestyle, holiness becomes your identity.

Reflection Questions

1. Do you radically obey when God speaks, or do you wrestle until your flesh is at peace with His instructions?
2. Are you someone who prefers occasional sacrifice over consistent obedience?

3. How is God inviting you into greater obedience and holiness today?

Prayer Focus

1. **Obedience**

Father, open my spiritual eyes to see as You see. Reveal the areas of my life and mindset that are not fully submitted to You. Give me the courage to respond with immediate obedience, even when it costs me something.

2. **Holiness**

Father, help me pursue radical obedience so the fruit of Your work in me is that I look more like You. Make my life a reflection of Your holiness in my speech, actions, and desires.

Key Takeaway: Holiness is not achieved by striving—it is birthed from radical obedience to God.

CHAPTER 4

The Fear of the Lord

(WEEK 1 - DAY 4)

The Beginning of Intimacy

You are already more than halfway through Week 1. That is a significant milestone, and it shows a hunger to go deeper. Today we pause to explore a truth often misunderstood: the fear of the Lord.

This fear is not about being terrified of God. Adam and Eve hid from Him after they sinned in the garden, consumed by shame and dread (Genesis 3:10). That type of fear drives us away from His presence. But holy fear is different. It is awe, reverence, and a deep desire never to be separated from Him.

Holy fear says: *"I cannot imagine life outside of Your presence."* It is the posture that bows low, recognizing God's majesty, sovereignty, and holiness. It is the kind of fear that draws us nearer, not farther away.

The Bible declares, *"The fear of the Lord is the beginning of knowledge, but fools despise wisdom and instruction"* (Proverbs 1:7 NIV). Without holy fear, we cannot truly know Him. Reverence opens the doorway to intimacy, wisdom, and transformation

Holy Fear Produces Radical Obedience

A healthy fear of the Lord makes us quick to obey because we value His voice above all others. It is the deep conviction that His approval matters more than the applause of man. Holy fear guards us against compromise. It reminds us that disobedience not only offends His holiness but also robs us of intimacy with Him.

John Bevere explains it well: *"The road to life has two ditches legalism and lawlessness. The love of God delivers us from legalism. The fear of the Lord delivers us from lawlessness."*

Holy fear brings balance: we love what He loves and hate what He hates (Proverbs 8:13). We don't obey to earn His love; we obey because we already have it and never want to lose the sweetness of His presence.

This is why Scripture often connects holy fear to obedience and blessing:

Blessed is the one who fears the Lord always – **Proverbs 28:14 ESV**

The fear of the Lord is a fountain of life, that one may turn away from the snares of death – **Proverbs 14:27 ESV**

The more we walk in reverence, the quicker we are to obey. Radical obedience flows naturally when the fear of the Lord governs our hearts.

The fear of the Lord in Daily Life

Holy fear should not be limited to just when in sacred spaces – it should shape every area of life.

- **In decisions**: Do you choose what is popular, or do you choose what honors God?
- **In relationships**: Are you more concerned about people's opinions than God's approval?
- **In hidden moments**: What do you watch, think, or do when no one else is looking?

Living with holy fear means living with the awareness that God sees all and that our lives are lived before His face. It is not about walking in dread of punishment but in a joyful reverence that says: *"Lord, I want my life to delight You."*

This is why Isaiah prophesied about Jesus, saying: *The Spirit of the Lord will rest on Him—the Spirit of wisdom and understanding, the Spirit of counsel and might, the Spirit of knowledge and the fear of the Lord. And He will delight in the fear of the Lord...* – Isaiah 11:2-3. Even Christ delighted in walking in holy reverence toward His Father.

Reflection Questions

1. Do you have a fear of the Lord?
2. Does what others think ever make you hesitate to obey God?
3. Do you pursue the validation of man more than the approval of God?

Prayer Focus

1. **Holy Fear**

   Father, give me a holy fear of You. Show me the ways I have lost reverence so I can repent. Show me where I have valued the validation of man over Your approval. Fill me with the Spirit of the fear of the Lord.

2. **Boldness and Audacity**

Give me courage to be bold and audacious for You in this season. Give me wisdom to navigate this world without compromising intimacy with You.

Key Takeaway: The fear of the Lord is not terror but reverence— loving Him so much that you never want to be away from Him.

CHAPTER 5

Surrender

(WEEK 1 - DAY 5)

Intimacy Requires Surrender

You have now reached Day 5 of the challenge, and the theme today is one of the most critical aspects of intimacy with God—surrender.

There is no intimacy without surrender. The more you release to Him, the deeper your intimacy grows. Holding onto control may feel safe, but it creates walls that keep His Presence at a distance.

Revelation 3:20 says, *"Here I am! I stand at the door and knock. If anyone hears my voice and opens the door, I will come in and eat with that person, and they with me."* God will not override your free will; He invites you to yield every area of your life to Him.

Think of surrender as the difference between inviting God into your living room versus giving Him access to every room in your house. True intimacy comes when you no longer keep certain areas locked away.

The Posture of Surrender

Surrender is not passive resignation; it is an active trust that God's way is best. Surrender looks like:

- *Releasing worry and anxiety.* Choosing to cast your cares on Him because He cares for you (1 Peter 5:7).
- *Being at peace with uncertainty.* Trusting Him when you can't see the outcome (Isaiah 26:3).
- *Remaining calm in storms.* Knowing God is in control and believing He is in the boat with you even when the storms rage (Mark 4:35–41).
- *Trusting the crushing.* Knowing that God brings beauty, wisdom, and oil out of seasons of pressure (2 Corinthians 4:8–9, 17).

But surrender is not easy. What often hinders us?

- *Pride* – Believing we know best or that we must stay in control.
- *Disappointment* – Past letdowns that make it hard to trust God again.
- *Trauma* – Deep wounds that keep us guarded and self-reliant.
- *Fear* – Worry that if we let go, God won't come through.

Yet God desires to meet us in these very places. He does not expose brokenness to shame us. He reveals it to redeem, heal, and restore. When we yield even the most painful parts of our lives, we give Him the opportunity to step in and be glorified in our story.

Surrender Unlocks Intimacy

Surrender is the foundation of intimacy because it creates room for God to be God. Without it, we reduce Him to a therapist we occasionally check in with rather than the Lord of our lives.

Jesus said, *"For whoever desires to save his life will lose it, but whoever loses his life for My sake will find it"* (Matthew 16:25 NKJV). In other words, the more we cling to control, the less we experience true life. But when we let go – when we surrender – we discover freedom, joy, and intimacy on a deeper level.

Proverbs 3:5-6 reminds us: *Trust in the Lord with all your heart, and lean not on your own understanding; in all your ways acknowledge Him, and He shall direct your paths.* Notice the progression: trust, release, acknowledge, and then direction. God leads clearly when we yield fully.

When you surrender:

- *Your mind* is renewed. You stop relying on your limited perspective.
- *Your heart* is healed. You give Him permission to touch broken places.
- *Your will* is aligned. You stop fighting His plans and begin to flow in His grace.

Surrender is not loss—it is the greatest gain. Surrender puts Jesus at the wheel of your life.

Reflection Questions

1. Are you fully surrendered to God, or are there areas you still hold back?
2. What is standing in the way of your surrender – pride, fear, disappointment, or past hurts?
3. What stories are you telling yourself to justify holding onto control?
4. What broken area do you need to invite God into today?

Prayer Focus

1. **Surrender**

   Father, I surrender all to You. Search me and reveal every area I have not fully given up. Heal every broken place so I can trust You completely. Be glorified in every part of my life, my family, my work, my ministry, and every hidden area of my heart

Key Takeaway: The depth of your intimacy with God is directly connected to the depth of your surrender. What you yield to Him becomes the place He fills with His presence.

CHAPTER 6

Help My Unbelief!

[WEEK 1 - DAY 6]

Faith and Unbelief Can Coexist

Day 6 invites us to deal with an honest truth: you can have faith and still wrestle with unbelief.

Faith is not static. It grows and strengthens – or it diminishes and weakens – depending on how we respond to life's circumstances. Victories tend to build our confidence, while setbacks and disappointments can erode it. The presence of faith doesn't automatically erase doubt, but it does give us the power to choose to trust God even when unbelief whispers in the background.

Mark 9 tells the story of a desperate father whose son was tormented by an unclean spirit. He cried out to Jesus, *"Lord, I believe; help my unbelief!"* (Mark 9:24 NKJV). That prayer was raw and vulnerable—an admission of faith and doubt coexisting. And Jesus didn't reject him for his weakness. Instead, He responded with compassion, healed the boy, and honored the man's imperfect but honest faith.

This shows us that God is not put off by our struggles with unbelief. What matters is that we bring them to Him. Faith, even if it's imperfect, still moves the heart of God when we are surrendered to Him.

But there is also a warning: unbelief left unchecked can choke out faith, turn us away from God thereby hindering His work in our lives (Hebrews 3:12). That is why it must be identified and uprooted.

The Subtle Danger of Unbelief

Unbelief often doesn't announce itself. It doesn't come knocking loudly drawing attention it itself. Instead, it creeps in quietly through disappointment, unanswered prayers, fear of failure, or prolonged waiting. Unbelief sounds like the internal voice of consolation when faith proves unfruitful. Unbelief sounds like:

- "Maybe this is not what God wants for me."
- "What's the point? Nothing is going to change."
- "Maybe I'm not good enough?"
- "I know He can, but I don't think He will."

The Israelites experienced this in the wilderness. Though they had seen God part the Red Sea and provide manna from heaven, they still doubted His ability to bring them into the Promised Land. Their unbelief cost them forty years in the desert (Numbers 14:22–23).

Unchecked unbelief can:

- *Delay destiny* – like Israel, we wander instead of entering God's promises.
- *Distort perspective* – causing us to magnify problems and minimize God's power.
- *Diminish intimacy* – because unbelief questions God's goodness and weakens trust.

This is why dealing with unbelief is essential for intimacy with God.

How to Deal with Unbelief

Unbelief is not something to ignore; it must be confronted and replaced with the truth of God. Here's how:

1. **Acknowledge it** – Like the father in Mark 9, admit where unbelief exists and repent. Honesty is the first step to healing.

    - *If we confess our sins, He is faithful and just and will forgive us our sins and purify us from all unrighteousness* – **1 John 1:9 NIV**

2. **Feed your faith** – Faith grows through the Word. Find scriptures about your situation, write them down, and meditate on them daily. Use them to pray.

    - *Faith comes by hearing, and hearing by the word of God* – **Romans 10:17 KJV**

3. **Reject lies** – Every thought that contradicts God's Word must be taken captive. It must be stopped in its tracks and replaced with truth.

    - *We take captive every thought to make it obedient to Christ* – **2 Corinthians 10:5 NIV**

4. **Confess life** – Speak God's Word over your life until faith rises. What you declare shapes what you believe.

    - *Death and life are in the power of the tongue, And those who love it will eat its fruit* – **Proverbs 18:21**

Faith grows when it is fed and exercised. Unbelief shrinks when it is starved. What you choose to focus on will determine which one wins.

The Reward of Faith

Even small faith has great power. Jesus said, *If you have faith as small as a mustard seed, you can say to this mountain, 'Move from here to there,' and it will move. Nothing will be impossible for you* – Matthew 17:20 NIV

Faith doesn't have to be perfect; it simply has to be alive and active. As you consistently feed your faith and confront unbelief, you will:

- Walk in greater peace, even when the outcome is uncertain.
- See prayers answered, even those that once felt out of reach.
- Experience deeper intimacy with God because you trust His character above your circumstances.

Reflection Questions

1. What types of faith does the Bible describe (little faith, great faith, growing faith etc)? Where are you on that spectrum?
2. In what areas are you wrestling with doubt, fear, or unbelief right now?
3. Where have you left unbelief unchecked and seen your faith diminish?
4. How can you practically "feed" your faith this week?

Prayer Focus

1. **Unbelief**

   Father, reveal every area of unbelief in my life. I repent of unbelief. Speak Your Word into these places and breathe life where faith has died. Restore what unbelief has stolen and bring divine acceleration in Jesus' name.

Key Takeaway: Faith and unbelief can coexist, but only one can rule. What you feed will grow—so starve unbelief and feed your faith until it overflows.

CHAPTER 7

In or Out

(WEEK 1 - DAY 7)

The Power of a Decision

You've made it to Day 7 – well done! Reaching this point shows not only perseverance but also hunger for God. Today is different though because it is decision day.

Every relationship requires commitment, and intimacy with God is no different. Jesus never invited His disciples to follow from the sidelines. He called them to leave everything and follow Him: *"Whoever wants to be my disciple must deny themselves and take up their cross and follow me"* (Matthew 16:24).

The question today is simple but life-changing: **Are you in or out?**

Many are willing to count the cost when pursuing earthly goals— working long hours for a promotion or extra income, sacrificing sleep to earn a degree, or enduring discomfort for fitness, health, even beauty. Yet, when it comes to pursuing intimacy with God, hesitation often creeps in. We convince ourselves we'll start tomorrow, when things settle down, or when life feels less demanding.

In Christ, there is no room for divided loyalties. God is looking for those who will say without hesitation, *"I'm all in."*

The Cost and the Reward

Choosing to go "all in" with God comes with a cost. Jesus warned His followers to count that cost: *"Suppose one of you wants to build a tower. Won't you first sit down and estimate the cost to see if you have enough money to complete it?"* – Luke 14:28 NIV

The cost may include:

- Rearranging your priorities to make space for God.
- Losing the approval of people when you choose obedience over popularity.
- Laying down personal ambitions to embrace His higher purpose.
- Saying no to temporary pleasures so you can say yes to eternal rewards.

But while the cost is real, the reward is far greater:

- **Deeper intimacy** – You experience the Presence of God like never before (James 4:8).
- **Clearer purpose** – You discover the assignment He created you for (Jeremiah 29:11).
- **Greater authority** – Your prayers carry weight because your life is fully aligned with Him (John 15:7).
- **Eternal impact** – You leave a legacy that echoes in heaven, because early treasures are temporary (Matthew 6:19–20).

God is raising an army of believers who will rise up and build, occupy, and fight back against the works of darkness. That begins with a firm decision: In or Out?

The Danger of Half-Heartedness

Indecision is a decision in itself. To waver between "in" and "out" is lukewarmness – the very state Jesus warns against: *Because you are lukewarm – neither hot nor cold – I am about to spit you out of my mouth* – Revelation 3:16 NIV.

Half-hearted Christianity looks like:

- Serving God when it's convenient.
- Worshipping Him in public but not having a personal worship and prayer life
- Giving Him parts of your life while keeping other areas off-limits.

But God is calling His people to unwavering devotion to Him. Joshua challenged Israel with this same decision: *Choose for yourselves this day whom you will serve… but as for me and my household, we will serve the Lord* – Joshua 24:15 NIV. The same call echoes to us today.

Reflection Questions

- What will it take for you to leave where you are and go deeper with God?
- What is God calling you to do for His Kingdom in this season?
- Are there areas where fear, comfort, or the opinion of others is holding you back from fully committing?
- What would it look like for you to say, "I am all in" today?

Prayer Focus

1. **Commitment**

   Father, I choose to be all in. I surrender every competing loyalty and every hesitation.

   Give me the courage to say yes to You completely, no matter the cost. Align my heart with Your purpose for my life and let my life testify that I belong fully to You.

Key Takeaway: Intimacy with God requires a decision. You cannot walk halfway with Him. The question is simple: Are you in or out?

WEEK 2

Be Still

CHAPTER 8

Be Still and Know

(WEEK 2 - DAY 8)

The Call to Stillness

Welcome to Week 2! You have pressed through the first week, and now God is inviting you to go deeper. The pace of life often drowns out God's voice. This week calls us to intentionally slow down and lean into His presence with one goal: **be still and know that He is God** (Psalm 46:10).

The Hebrew word for *"be still"* is *raphah*, meaning to relax, let go, or sink down. It paints the picture of loosening your grip, of no longer striving or fighting in your own strength. Stillness is not laziness; it is an intentional posture of surrender and quiet trust.

The word *"know"* in Hebrew is *yada,* which means to intimately experience, to encounter, or to understand through relationship—not just intellectual acknowledgment. To "be still and know" is to restfully surrender into His presence and experience Him at a deeper level.

Stillness positions us to:

- Hear God's voice more clearly.
- Encounter His Peace in a chaotic world.
- Experience His Presence as a refuge and strength.

When we practice stillness, we declare with our posture what our lips may not yet have the words to say: *"You are God, and I am not."*

The Challenge of StillnessBeing still is not easy in a noisy world. Phones, schedules, constant notifications, and endless to-do lists make stillness feel unnatural – even uncomfortable. Many of us are more at ease with busyness than with quiet.

Yet intimacy with God often requires silence before Him—both *external quiet* and *internal stillness*.

- *External stillness:* Creating an environment free from distraction. This might mean turning off your phone, closing your laptop – no multi-tasking, or stepping outside into nature.
- *Internal stillness:* Quieting the noise within—worries, anxieties, racing thoughts, and endless planning. It means handing over mental clutter and focusing your heart on being in His Presence.

God told Moses, *"My presence will go with you, and I will give you rest"* (Exodus 33:14). Rest is not the absence of activity; it is found in the presence of the Lord.

When we let go of control and acknowledge God as the center of our lives, we discover Him in deeper ways. Stillness reminds us that we are not the ones holding everything together—He is. Only then can we say with confidence, *"The Lord is my refuge and strength, an ever-present help in trouble"* (Psalm 46:1).

The Fruit of Stillness

When you practice stillness, something shifts within you. The more you still yourself before Him, the more you begin to notice:

- **Peace replacing anxiety**. His Presence calms fears, anxious thoughts, and brings supernatural rest (Philippians 4:6–7).
- **Clarity in confusion**. What once felt complicated becomes clear when His voice cuts through the noise (Isaiah 30:21).
- **Strength in weakness**. As you stop striving, His power is made perfect in your weakness (2 Corinthians 12:9).
- **Joy in His presence**. As Psalm 16:11 (NIV) says, *"You will fill me with joy in Your presence, with eternal pleasures at Your right hand."*

Stillness is not wasted time—it is invested time. It is in stillness that we are renewed, recalibrated, and reminded of who He is and who we are in Him.

Reflection Questions

1. When was the last time you intentionally sat still before God without agenda or distraction?
2. What distracts you most from resting in His presence—noise, busyness, fear, or something else?
3. What would it look like for you to regularly practice stillness and surrender this week?
4. How might your relationship with God deepen if you consistently created space to be still?

Prayer Focus

1. **Stillness**

   Lord, teach me to be still and know that You are God. Quiet my heart from striving, silence my anxious thoughts, and bring rest to my weary soul. Help me to release control and lean fully into Your presence. May I encounter Your peace, clarity, and strength as I wait in stillness before You.

   Key Takeaway: Stillness is not inactivity—it is active trust. When we quiet ourselves before God, we make room for His voice and His peace.

CHAPTER 9

The Presence of God

[WEEK 2 - DAY 9]

Pursue His Presence

Day 9 focuses on one of the greatest treasures available to us: the Presence of God.

Pursuing His presence is not optional for intimacy – it is foundational. Everything flows from His presence. Without it, worship becomes performance, prayer becomes ritual, and life becomes dry and powerless.

God's presence is not just an atmosphere we enter on Sunday mornings. It is a lifestyle—moment-by-moment awareness of Him, wherever we are.

As believers, we are called to pursue and guard His presence jealously, making it a priority over everything else.

David understood this. He was a man passionate about the presence of God. He declared in Psalm 16:11 (NLT), *"You will show me the way of life, granting me the joy of Your presence and the pleasures of living with You forever."* In His Presence we discover the very way of life and obtain the joys of living and walking with God. His Presence is not just a gift for it is necessary for survival.

God's presence is not confined to an atmosphere we enter on Sunday mornings. It is not limited to a church building or service. Pursuing His Presence is a lifestyle – moment-by-moment awareness that He is with us wherever we are. We can fellowship with Him at anytime.

As believers, we are called to pursue and guard His Presence jealously, making it the priority above every other pursuit.

How to Enter His Presence

God has given us a pattern for approaching Him. Psalm 100 outlines a roadmap to enter His Presence:

- **Make a joyful noise.** Joy is an expression of confidence in who God is, not just in how life feels. Joy is an act of faith, not just an emotion. It is a declaration that God is God, regardless of circumstances. Paul and Silas sang praises in prison (Acts 16:25), and God responded with freedom and victory. Joy helps us enter His presence and disarms the enemy.
- **Come before Him with singing.** Worshipping with song shifts the atmosphere. Singing is not about musical ability but about posture of heart. When we lift our voices, we proclaim God's greatness above our situation. Psalm 22:3 tells us God inhabits the praises of His people – He literally makes His dwelling among those who sing His praise.
- **Enter His gates with thanksgiving.** Gratitude is the key that opens the gate. Thanksgiving acknowledges what God has already done and builds faith for what He will do. Like the leper who returned to give thanks in Luke 17:15–16, thanksgiving positions us to see greater manifestation of God's glory.

- **Enter His courts with praise.** Praise exalts His name above circumstances and magnifies His greatness. Praise is different from thanksgiving. Thanksgiving looks back at what He has done; praise looks up at who He is. Praise magnifies God's character, reminding us of His majesty, power, and sovereignty. The more we praise, the smaller our problems appear compared to His greatness.
- **Bless His name.** The Hebrew word for bless in that verse is *barak* which means to kneel in adoration, recognizing His holiness and sovereignty. This act of humility acknowledges His holiness and exalts Him in our lives as Lord of all.

The Fruit of His Presence

The result of dwelling in His presence is always **transformation.** You cannot be before the Almighty and remain the same.

In His presence, you will find that:

- **Joy fills the soul** and sustains through trials. *"In Your presence is fullness of joy"* (Psalm 16:11 NKJV).
- **Rest quiets the heart** and refreshes our soul. *"My presence will go with you, and I will give you rest"* (Exodus 33:14 NIV).
- **Revelation flows freely** and illuminates our path *"Call to Me, and I will answer you, and show you great and mighty things, which you do not know."* (Jeremiah 33:3 NKJV).

The Presence of God is vital to the spiritual life of every believer – it is the very air we breathe. Without it we suffocate and die

Reflection Questions

1. Do you leave prayer still feeling burdened or anxious? Could it be you haven't truly entered His presence?
2. What hinders you most from entering the Presence of the Lord?
3. What unique practices help you stay in His presence daily?
4. How would your daily life change if you pursued His presence as faithfully as you pursue work, family, or goals?

Prayer Focus

1. **Presence of God**

   Father, remove every hindrance that keeps me from entering Your presence fully. Teach me the unique ways You have designed me to meet with You. Help me restructure my life so that Your presence is my highest priority. May joy, rest, and revelation flow as I dwell with You daily.

Key Takeaway: Pursuing the Presence of God is a lifestyle to cultivate. In His presence you find joy, rest, comfort, and revelation that nothing in this world can replace. Pursue it and guard it intently.

CHAPTER 10

The Voice of God

(WEEK 2 - DAY 10)

Hearing God Clearly

Welcome to Day 10! By now, you've been pressing deeper into intimacy with the Lord, and today we come to one of the most vital aspects of walking with Him: *hearing His voice.*

Think about it – what is intimacy without communication? You can't claim closeness with God if you don't recognize His voice. Jesus said it plainly: *"My sheep hear my voice, and I know them, and they follow me.."* (John 10:27 KJV).

Hearing the voice of God is vital in the life of a child of God. It gives direction when you don't know which way to turn. It brings correction when you're about to wander off the path. It offers encouragement when your soul feels weary. It breathes life into dry places.

But here's the challenge: we live in a world full of competing voices – our own anxious thoughts, the opinions and pressures of others, and yes, the lies of the enemy. If you are not intentional about learning to discern God's voice, you will end up confused, distracted, and led astray.

This is why intimacy demands clarity. And clarity comes from knowing the difference between God's voice, your voice, and the enemy's voice.

Discerning God's Voice

God is always speaking – but the question is: are you tuned in?

He speaks in many ways, including:

- **Through Scripture.** God speaks through His Word. If you want to hear Him, start reading your Bible. Every impression, voice, thought, dream, or prophecy must pass through the filter of His Word. The Bible is the unchanging, inerrant Word of God. God does not contradict His Word because that would make Him a liar. Numbers 23:19 tells us He is incapable of lying. So, if you need guidance or direction for your life, it is found in His Word. Psalm 119:105 says, *"Your word is a lamp to guide my feet and a light for my path."* If you want to hear God concerning an issue but ignoring the Word, you're missing the loudest way He speaks.
- **Through the Holy Spirit's inner prompting**. This is the *still small voice* Elijah heard in 1 Kings 19:12. It may be a nudge to call someone, a conviction about a decision, or a quiet reassurance in your spirit. The more you respond to these promptings, the more sensitive you become to them. Ignoring them dulls your spiritual hearing.
- **Through dreams and visions**. Just as God spoke to Joseph about his future (Genesis 37) and to Daniel with visions of things to come (Daniel 7), He still speaks through supernatural encounters today.
- **Through circumstances**. Sometimes doors opening or closing are not random – they are God's way of guiding you. Divine appointments, delays, or even obstacles can

all be how God speaks to lead you in a specific direction (Proverbs 16:9). Discernment is needed here, because not every open door is from God, but He can use circumstances to position you exactly where He needs you to be.

- **Through creation and nature.** Psalm 19:1 declares, *"The heavens proclaim the glory of God. The skies display his craftsmanship."* The beauty of a sunrise, the stillness of the ocean, or the order of creation itself can all be reminders of His majesty. Sometimes God uses what He has made to realign our perspective and remind us of His greatness.

- **Through people**. God often uses others to confirm what He's been speaking. This can be through godly counsel, prophetic voices, or even unexpected conversations. Proverbs 11:14 says, *"Without wise leadership, a nation falls; there is safety in having many advisers."* But note: people should confirm what God has already placed in your heart, not replace His voice in your life.

But here's the safeguard: *His voice never contradicts His Word or His character.* If what you think you're hearing goes against Scripture, it is not Him. If it stirs fear, shame, or condemnation, it's not Him. God's voice brings conviction, not condemnation; peace, not chaos; clarity, not confusion.

And here's another truth we often avoid: unresolved wounds can distort what you hear. If you're still carrying trauma, offense, disappointment, or bitterness, your filter is clouded. Instead of hearing clearly, you hear through the lens of your pain. That's why healing is not optional if you want intimacy. God wants to heal your heart so His voice can flow without distortion.

How to Position Yourself to Hear

If you want to hear God clearly, you must posture yourself intentionally.

1. **Be still.** Silence the noise. God's voice is often drowned out by busyness and distraction (Psalm 46:10).
2. **Stay in the Word.** The more you know His Word, the more you recognize His voice.
3. **Stay pure in heart.** Sin, unforgiveness, and pride clog your spiritual ears. Repentance realigns you back to Him.
4. **Test what you hear.** Test every word, thought, feeling, prophesy against Scripture. If it doesn't align, dismiss it (1 Thessalonians 5:21).
5. **Practice obedience.** The more you obey what you hear, the clearer His voice becomes. Disobedience dulls your ability to hear God; obedience sharpens it.

Reflection Questions

1. How do you currently discern God's voice in your life?
2. Are there unresolved hurts or distractions that may be distorting what you hear?
3. What steps can you take to deepen your ability to hear God's voice clearly?
4. Do you value His voice above the opinions of people, or do you let outside noise guide your choices?

Prayer Focus

1. **Voice of God**

   Father, remove every hindrance that keeps me from hearing You clearly. Expose every deception of the enemy and silence every counterfeit voice. Heal areas of brokenness, trauma, or fear that distort what I hear. Sharpen my spiritual senses to recognize Your voice quickly and to obey without hesitation.

Key Takeaway: God is always speaking—our part is to quiet competing voices, lean into His Word, and obey what He says.

CHAPTER 11

Intercession

(WEEK 2 - DAY 11)

The Power of Intercession

Today, we are talking about intercession and prophecy because the more intimate are with God, the more He reveals His heart to us. Just as we go before Him and share the burdens of our hearts, God begins to share the burdens of His heart concerning people, families, situations, and even nations. Sometimes, He calls us to partner with Him in carrying that burden.

Intercession is not just prayer – it is *standing in the gap* and taking on the role of mediator on behalf of others. When you intercede, you are not just praying *for* someone but you're are seeking the will (desire) of the Father and praying to see it is fulfilled.

Ezekiel 22:30 gives us a sobering picture of God's desire: *"I looked for someone who might rebuild the wall of righteousness that guards the land. I searched for someone to stand in the gap in the wall so I wouldn't have to destroy the land, but I found no one"*. Intercession is answering that call – it is becoming the one who stands in the gap so destruction can be averted and God's mercy released.

To intercede effectively, you must know God's heart. And His heart is revealed through His Word. This is why Scripture is not just helpful but essential in intercession. You are not praying your opinions or desires; you are praying His will. When you declare Scripture over a person, family, or situation, you are aligning earth with heaven.

Examples of intercession:

- *Abraham* interceding for Sodom and Lot (Genesis 18).
- *Moses* pleading with God to spare Israel after their rebellion (Exodus 32:11–14).
- *Jesus* Himself, who intercedes for us continually before the Father (Hebrews 7:25 NLT).

Intercession is sacrificial, it is powerful, and it shifts atmospheres.

Prophecy and Discernment

God still speaks today. One of the ways He does this is through prophecy—when He releases direction, encouragement, or correction through His Spirit. Paul encouraged the early church: *"Let love be your highest goal! But you should also desire the special abilities the Spirit gives—especially the ability to prophesy"* (1 Corinthians 14:1 NLT).

Prophecy, however, requires discernment. We live in a world filled with voices—our own, others', the enemy's, and God's. Without discernment, we risk mistaking a counterfeit voice for the voice of God.

Here are key safeguards for prophecy:

- **Scripture first**. If a word contradicts God's Word, it is not from Him. "For You have magnified Your word above all Your name" (Psalm 138:2).

- **God's character**. Prophecy should sound like the heart of God—full of love, truth, and clarity. It may bring conviction, but it will not produce condemnation, fear, or confusion.
- **Confirmation.** True prophecy often confirms what God has already been stirring in someone's heart. It should never manipulate or control.
- **Fruit**. Look at the outcome. Does the word produce peace, faith, and alignment with God's will, or does it produce chaos and distraction?

When prophecy flows from a place of intimacy and intercession, it carries weight. It doesn't flatter—it builds. It doesn't confuse—it clarifies. It doesn't exalt man—it points to Jesus.

To walk in prophetic discernment, you must cultivate:

- A pure heart before God (Matthew 5:8).
- A renewed mind grounded in His Word (Romans 12:2).
- Sensitivity to the Holy Spirit's leading (John 16:13).

Reflection Questions

1. How comfortable are you with interceding for others?
2. Do you believe God wants to use you prophetically to strengthen, encourage, and comfort others? Why or why not?
3. How can you sharpen your discernment to test what you hear against God's Word and His character?
4. What step can you take this week to strengthen both your prayer life and your prophetic sensitivity?

Prayer Focus

1. **Intercession**

   Father, as I draw nearer to you, help me to hear your voice clearly. Silence every distraction and every voice that is not yours. Heal the broken areas of my heart and life that twist and distort what you are saying. Give me a burden for the things that burden your heart. Reveal to me in the place of prayer who you want me to intercede for and how you want me to pray concerning them.

Key Takeaway: Intercession and prophecy flow from intimacy with the Father.

CHAPTER 12

God's Voice: His Word

(WEEK 2 - DAY 12)

The Word as God's Voice

Welcome to Day 12! Today I want to remind you that the Word of God is the voice of God.

I know I have said this several times already during this challenge but I keep coming back to it because it is key:

Engaging with God's Word is essential for intimacy. Without it, our ability to hear Him clearly becomes compromised because His Word is the primary filter through which every other "voice" must be tested.

All creation exists today because God spoke His Word, and that word is alive and active.

Jesus said in John 6:63 (NIV), *"The words I have spoken to you—they are full of the Spirit and life."*

The Word is not just ink on paper—it is Spirit-breathed, alive, and active.

Hebrews 4:12 declares: *"For the word of God is alive and powerful. It is sharper than the sharpest two-edged sword, cutting between soul and spirit, between joint and marrow. It exposes our innermost thoughts and desires"*.

Every time you open Scripture, you are encountering His voice, His nature, and His promises. This is why the Word must be central in your pursuit of intimacy with Him. Without it, your ability to hear Him clearly becomes compromised.

When you neglect the Word, you risk being deceived by emotions, culture, or the enemy. But when you are rooted in the Word, you have a firm foundation that is not easily shaken.

Isaiah 55:11 (NIV) says this about God's word, *so is my word that goes out from my mouth: It will not return to me empty, but will accomplish what I desire and achieve the purpose for which I sent it.*

This is a reminder of just how powerful God's Word is!

It will never come back empty but will accomplish the very thing God desires and the purpose for which He sent it. Now imagine the authority you walk in when, in the place of intimacy, you discern His desire concerning a matter and then release His Word on assignment to fulfill it.

The reason many of us don't see results is because we're trying to send His Word on assignment for *our* desires instead of His.

Why the Word Matters

The Word of God is not optional—it is essential. Here's why:

1. **The Word gives life.**

    The Word quickens your spirit, renews your mind, and strengthens your inner man. It breathes hope into dry places. Jeremiah 15:16 says, *"When I discovered your words, I devoured them. They are my joy and my heart's delight."*

2. **The Word is powerful.**

    From creation itself, the Word demonstrated its authority: *"God said, 'Let there be light,' and there was light"* (Genesis 1:3). Everything in existence came through His Word, and nothing exists apart from it (John 1:3). When you declare His Word, you are releasing creative, sustaining power into your situation.

3. **The Word is reliable.**

    Unlike shifting emotions or circumstances, the Word stands unshaken. Psalm 138:2 says, *"For you have magnified Your Word above all Your name"* (NKJV). That means God binds Himself to His Word—it cannot fail. Numbers 23:19 reminds us, *"God is not a man, that He should lie... Has He ever spoken and failed to act?"*

4. **The Word transforms.**

    Romans 12:2 teaches us that transformation comes by the renewing of our minds. As you read, meditate, and apply the Word, your thinking shifts, your desires align with His, and your life begins to reflect Him.

5.   **The Word equips.**

2 Timothy 3:16–17 says Scripture is God-breathed and equips us for every good work. Intimacy with God is not just about experiencing Him but also being prepared to serve Him. The Word arms you with wisdom, discernment, and strength for every season.

Engaging the Word Daily

To treat Scripture casually is to treat God's voice casually. If you only rely on sermons or Sunday services, your spiritual life will remain malnourished. *Daily engagement with the Word is non-negotiable for intimacy.*

Here are practical ways to engage His Word:

- **Read it.** Set aside time every day to read the Bible.
- **Meditate on it.** Choose a verse or passage to dwell on throughout the day. Ask the Holy Spirit to speak to you about that verse or passage.
- **Pray it.** Turn Scripture into prayer. Declare His promises over your life and family.
- **Memorize it.** Hide His Word in your heart so the Holy Spirit can bring it to mind when you need it most (Psalm 119:11).
- **Obey it.** Revelation without application is useless. The blessing is found in applying the Word, not just hearing it (James 1:22).

Reflection Questions

1. How often do you engage with the Word of God outside of Sunday service?
2. What distractions keep you from consistent Bible reading, and how can you remove them?
3. What practices—reading, journaling, memorization, or praying Scripture—help you connect with God's Word most deeply
4. What changes can you make to engage the Word daily and hear God's voice more clearly?

Prayer Focus

1. **Voice of God**

   Father, stir up a deep hunger for Your Word in me. Remove every distraction, excuse, or hindrance that keeps me from studying your Word. Open my eyes to see You in every page. Let Your Word come alive to me bringing clarity, direction, and transformation. Teach me and give me the grace to do what your Word says.

Key Takeaway: The Word of God is His voice to you today—read it, meditate on it, and live by it.

CHAPTER 13

The Enemy's Voice

[WEEK 2 - DAY 13]

Recognizing the Counterfeit

Day 13 brings us face-to-face with a critical truth: *the enemy has a voice, and it can sound dangerously similar to God's voice.*

At the root of Satan's rebellion was his desire to be God. That same pride fuels his tactics today – he attempts to *mimic* God, twist His Word, and distort His truth in order to deceive.

In Matthew 4, when Jesus was led into the wilderness, the enemy quoted Scripture. But he quoted it out of context, with the intent to trap Jesus into disobedience. If Satan tried to deceive the Son of God with Scripture, how much more must we be discerning as His followers?

Here's the difference: *God's voice brings life. The enemy's voice brings death.*

- God convicts with love; the enemy condemns with shame.
- God's voice calls you forward; the enemy's voice pulls you backward.

- God's voice leads you to freedom; the enemy's voice leads you to bondage.

The enemy's voice often carries *condemnation, guilt, discouragement, and shame.* It robs joy, kills peace, and drains spiritual energy. Left unchallenged, it will keep you stuck in cycles of fear and defeat.

In contrast, the voice of God—even when correcting – always carries hope. His conviction is wrapped in love, leading you toward repentance and restoration. His voice will never strip away your identity in Christ; it will always call you deeper into it.

How to Identify the Enemy's Voice

Learning to distinguish voices is essential for intimacy with God. Jesus said His sheep know His voice and *"a stranger's voice they will not follow"* (John 10:5). That means the more familiar you become with God's Word and His ways, the easier it is to detect the counterfeit.

Here are three safeguards:

1. **Check the fruit.**

    Jesus said, *"By their fruit you will recognize them"* (Matthew 7:20 NIV). Ask yourself: What is this voice producing in me? Peace or fear? Encouragement or despair? Life or death? God's voice will bear fruit consistent with His Spirit— love, joy, peace, patience, kindness, goodness, faithfulness, gentleness, and self-control (Galatians 5:22–23).

2. **Test it with Scripture.**

    The enemy loves to misquote, twist, or isolate verses to serve his deception. This is why we need the whole counsel of God's Word. If what you're hearing contradicts or takes

God's Word out of context, reject it immediately. Truth doesn't change based on feelings, circumstances, or culture.

3.   **Discern the source.**

Jesus described the thief's agenda in John 10:10: *"The thief comes only to steal and kill and destroy."* If the thought or voice you're hearing is draining your life, stealing your identity, or killing your destiny, it is not from God. His voice always aligns with His character as a good Shepherd who came to give life and life abundantly.

Breaking Agreement with Lies

One of the enemy's greatest strategies is to whisper lies until we agree with them. The enemy will present facts as though they were Truth. The moment you believe a lie, you empower the liar. But freedom comes when you recognize and reject the lie, then replace it with God's Truth.

- The enemy says: *"You'll never change."*
  God says: *"If anyone is in Christ, they are a new creation"* (2 Corinthians 5:17).
- The enemy says: *"You're not enough."*
  God says: *"You are more than a conqueror through Christ"* (Romans 8:37).
- The enemy says: *"God can never love you after what you have done."*
  God says: *"Nothing can separate you from My love"* (Romans 8:38–39).
- The enemy says: *"You've missed your chance; it's too late for you."*
  God says: *"God causes everything to work together for the good of those who love God and are called according to his purpose."* (Romans 8:28)

Victory comes when you replace lies with Truth. Don't just silence the enemy—overcome him with the Word of God, just as Jesus did in the wilderness.

Reflection Questions

1. What lies have you believed that have produced shame, guilt, or discouragement?
2. Which Scriptures directly confront those lies with Truth?
3. How can you build a habit of testing every voice you hear against God's Word?
4. What steps can you take to sharpen your discernment so you immediately recognize the lie?

Prayer Focus

1. **Lies of the Enemy**

   Father, expose every lie of the enemy that I have believed. Expose every area of shame, condemnation, and guilt. Reveal the thoughts, spoken words, and actions behind them that I need to repent of. Forgive me for everything I have thought, said, or done that has brought me out of alignment with your Truth. Help me to stand firm in Your promises and reject every counterfeit word from the enemy in Jesus' name.

Key Takeaway: The enemy's voice is subtle but destructive. Learn to test the voices you hear, reject the lie, and stand firm on God's Truth

CHAPTER 14

Silence

(WEEK 2 - DAY 14)

The Call to Silence

You've entered the home stretch – 7 more days left in this journey! Today's focus is one that feels foreign to many believers: silence.

Silence is not weakness, laziness, or absence—it is a spiritual discipline. In a world addicted to noise, scrolling, busyness, and constant chatter, silence feels strange and even uncomfortable. But it is in silence that we encounter the depths of God's presence.

Psalm 46:10 says, "Be still, and know that I am God." Stillness and silence are not optional when pursuing intimacy with the Father; they are the doorways to revelation. Silence teaches us to step back, stop striving, and allow God to be God.

Silence as Prayer

Prayer is often equated with words, but sometimes the most powerful prayers are the ones without them. There are moments when our hearts are too burdened, our emotions too raw, or our language too limited to capture what we need to say. In those moments, *silence becomes prayer.*

Romans 8:26 reminds us: *"The Holy Spirit helps us in our weakness. For example, we don't know what God wants us to pray for. But the Holy Spirit prays for us with groanings that cannot be expressed in words."*

Silence before God is not an empty void – it is *space for the Holy Spirit to intercede.* The Father hears what your mind has no words for.

Consider Hannah in 1 Samuel 1:13. She poured out her heart to God silently; her lips moved, but her voice was not heard. Yet God answered her prayer with the gift of Samuel. Silence did not lessen her prayer—it amplified it.

When we practice silence as prayer, we acknowledge that God, the One who searches our innermost being and knows our deepest thoughts, is the only one that is able to hear and answer our heart's cry. Our silence becomes trust. Our silence becomes surrender.

Silence as Praise

Silence can also be worship.

Psalm 65:1 (MSG) says, *"Silence is praise to you, Zion-dwelling God."* Praise is not always loud songs, lifted hands, or shouted hallelujahs. Sometimes the deepest praise is to fall silent before His majesty in awe and reverence.

There are moments when words feel inadequate. What could we possibly say in the face of His holiness that would be enough? In those moments, silence itself becomes adoration.

This kind of silence is not passive—it is a posture of the heart. It is bowing low in worship without saying a word, because the heart itself is crying out: *"Worthy is the Lamb."*

Silence as Listening

Silence is also the posture of **listening.** Too often, prayer is one-sided—we pour out our requests, our worries, and our desires, but never stop to let Him respond. True intimacy requires conversation, and conversation means listening as much as speaking.

There are two dimensions of silence you must learn to cultivate:

1. **External silence.** This is about creating a quiet environment—turning off your phone, stepping away from the noise, and entering your secret place. It's choosing solitude to make space to hear His voice.
2. **Internal silence.** This is more difficult. It is quieting the noise within—your racing thoughts, anxieties, fears, and endless planning. Internal silence does not mean emptying your mind (as in eastern meditation), but **filling your mind with Him and His Word.**

Only when both external and internal silence are cultivated can we clearly hear His whisper.

Elijah in 1 Kings 19:12, did not encounter God in the wind, earthquake, or fire. He encountered Him in the gentle whisper. The noise of life often drowns out that whisper, but when we practice silence, we tune our hearts to His frequency.

Reflection Questions:

1. Have you learned to see silence as prayer and worship, or do you still equate intimacy only with words?
2. Are there areas of your life where internal noise—fear, anxiety, busyness—has drowned out God's whisper?
3. Have you unknowingly practiced forms of silence that imitate eastern meditation instead of biblical stillness? If so, repent
4. What would it look like for you to intentionally practice silence before God this week?

Prayer Focus:

1. **Quiet the Noise**

   Father, quiet the noise in my mind and in my heart. Teach me to be still before You. Remove every distraction, fear, and anxious thought that crowds out Your voice. Help me to hear You clearly in the silence. Teach me to embrace stillness as worship, as prayer, and as intimacy with You.

WEEK 3

Go Deep

CHAPTER 15

Breaking Patterns

(WEEK 3 - DAY 15)

Recognizing Patterns

Welcome to Week 3! Today's focuses on identifying and breaking negative patterns in our lives, families, and even bloodlines. You cannot break what you refuse to recognize. Many of us live with recurring issues – patterns that keep showing up in our personal lives, our families, even in our bloodlines.

Some patterns are easy to spot:

- Cycles of fear that paralyze progress.
- Poverty or lack that seems to follow from generation to generation.
- Anger and broken relationships that destroy trust.
- Addictions that enslave and repeat themselves in family history.

Others are more subtle:

- Compromise in small areas that slowly weakens faith.
- Unbelief that quietly shuts the door on God's promises.

- Procrastination or delay that keeps you circling the same mountain instead of moving forward.

Patterns are not just habits—they are often spiritual in nature. They can be reinforced by negative thought cycles, repeated behaviors, or generational influences passed down through family lines. But here is the good news: *Christ has redeemed us from every curse* (Galatians 3:13). His blood breaks cycles. His Spirit transforms patterns. His Word renews the mind and establishes a new way of living.

Why Patterns Matter

Patterns left unchecked will always repeat. What you don't confront you can't conquer, and what you tolerate will dominate.

The Israelites are a sobering example. They wandered in the wilderness for 40 years because of a pattern of murmuring and disobedience. Instead of entering into their promised land, they wandered in the wilderness. What should have taken days ended up taking decades.

Unbroken patterns do the same in our lives today. They:

- *Delay progress.* You remain stuck instead of advancing into destiny.
- *Hinder intimacy.* Patterns of distraction, compromise, or sin make it harder to hear God clearly.
- *Affect future generations.* What is not confronted, surrendered, healed is inadvertently passed down to the next generation.

But patterns can be broken! As you walk closely with the Father, your perspective begins to align with His. Holy Spirit gives you insight and revelation, uncovering the patterns in your life that hinder growth and prevent victory.

Reflection Questions

1. What patterns—personal or generational—do you see in your life?
2. Have you noticed recurring areas of struggle, failure, or delay?
3. Are you tolerating cycles God has already given you authority to break?
4. What steps will you take to break these patterns through prayer, fasting, and accountability?

Prayer Focus

1. **Breaking Patterns**

   Father, reveal every negative pattern in my life and family. By the blood of Jesus, break cycles of fear, failure, sin, and delay. I break every agreement with generational cycles and patterns in my bloodline. Renew and restore my life back to your original design and intent. Establish new patterns of faith, obedience, victory in my life. Let me life testify to your Word that old things have passed away and all things have been made new in Christ.

Key Takeaway: Patterns can persist for generations, but through Christ you have authority to break negative cycles

CHAPTER 16

You are in a War

[WEEK 3 - DAY 16]

Spiritual Warfare is Real

As we enter this final stretch of the intimacy challenge, it is vital to remember: **you are in a spiritual war.**

Apostle Paul reminds us: *"For though we live in the world, we do not wage war as the world does"* (2 Corinthians 10:3). This war is not fought with physical weapons, but with spiritual ones. Your fight is not against people, but against unseen forces that oppose God's plan for your life (Ephesians 6:12).

The enemy's mission is simple yet devastating: *"The thief comes only to steal and kill and destroy"* (John 10:10). He wants to steal your intimacy with God, kill your destiny, and destroy anything good in your life.

But Christ has already won the ultimate victory at the cross. The second half of John 10:10 gives us the hope we stand on: *"I have come that they may have life, and have it to the full."*

Here's the truth: the closer you walk with God, the more resistance you will face. Spiritual warfare intensifies when intimacy deepens. Why? Because you are becoming more dangerous to the kingdom of darkness. Expect distractions. Expect discouragement. Expect pressure. But also expect victory, because God has armed you with weapons that cannot fail: *His armor* (Ephesians 6:10-18), *His Word, prayer, fasting, worship*

Worship as a Weapon

Worship is one of the most underestimated weapons of warfare. It is not the music selection before a sermon – it is a lifestyle that proclaims the supremacy of God

Romans 12:1 calls us to *"offer your bodies as a living sacrifice, holy and pleasing to God—this is your true and proper worship."* True worship is the posture of a surrendered life.

When you worship in the middle of battle, you:

- **Shift your perspective.** Instead of magnifying your problem, you magnify your God.
- **Shift the atmosphere.** Darkness cannot remain in the presence of light.
- **Silence fear.** Faith rises as you declare to glory and majesty of God.
- **Invite divine strategy.** Worship draws God into the fight and provokes His intervention.

Worship dethrones fear and enthrones Christ in your heart. It invites Man of war into the battle. It is how you take your stand in the middle of the storm.

The Power of Worship in Battle

Throughout Scripture, we see where worship was used as a strategy for victory.

- **Joshua 6** – The walls of Jericho did not fall by human might but by obedience and worship. Marching, trumpets, and a shout of praise brought supernatural breakthrough.
- **2 Chronicles 20** – Jehoshaphat's army was outnumbered, but he put singers at the front of the battle line. As they worshiped, the Lord set ambushes against their enemies, and Judah never had to lift a sword.
- **Acts 16** – Paul and Silas were praying and singing hymns to the Lord when an earthquake shook the foundations of the prison. Prison doors miraculously opened and their chains fell off.

Worship truly confuses the enemy—just look at 2 Chronicles 20. To worship in the middle of trials and challenges is to declare total dependence on God's power to save and deliver. That posture is both powerful and threatening to the enemy, because it means he no longer has a hold on you. Satan thrives on fear, but when you place your complete trust and surrender in God, his power is stripped away.

The Seven Types of Praise

Scripture outlines seven Hebrew words for praise—each with a different dimension of power. Together, they form a complete arsenal of weapons in the midst of a battle:

1. **Towdah** – Sacrificial praise, being a living sacrifice to God (Romans 12:1).
2. **Yadah** – The lifting of hands; declaring one's dependence on God and proclaiming love for Him (Exodus 17:11).

3. **Barak** – Bowing; giving reverence to God, recognizing His holiness and sovereignty (Psalm 5:7).
4. **Shabach** – Shouting loudly in triumph and faith; "shout"; lifting up your voice to praise God with all one's might (Psalm 47:1; Isaiah 12:6).
5. **Zamar** – Singing and playing instruments; expressing joy in the presence of the Lord (Psalm 150:3–5).
6. **Halal** – where we get Hallelujah – expressed as celebration; expressing praise through physical motion/ dance (2 Samuel 6:14).
7. **Tehillah** – The combination of all forms of praise, the fullness of worship (Psalm 22:25).

These expressions are not just symbolic—they are prophetic acts. Every act of worship is a declaration: *God has the final say in my situation.*

Reflection Questions

1. What spiritual battles are you currently facing in your life, family, or destiny?
2. How does your worship look when you are under pressure – is it strong or nonexistent?
3. Are you relying on your own strength, or are you following God's battle strategies through prayer, worship, and obedience?
4. What would it look like to fully trust God and worship through every problem this week?

Prayer Focus

1. **Grace to Endure and Win the War**

   Lord, thank You for training my hands for war and my fingers for battle. Give me grace to endure, strength to submit to Your process, and courage to obey Your strategies. Cancel every assignment of delay, sabotage, or destruction. Let my worship confuse the enemy and invite Your presence into every battle. In Jesus' name, Amen.

Key Takeaway: You are in a spiritual war, but Christ has already won the victory. Worship, prayer, and obedience are your powerful weapons.

CHAPTER 17

Worship as a Weapon

Worship Changes the Battle

Worship doesn't just prepare you for battle—**it changes the battle itself.**

When King Jehoshaphat faced impossible odds—three armies marching against Judah—he didn't send his best warriors first. He sent singers and worshippers. Scripture records: *"As they began to sing and praise, the Lord set ambushes against the men of Ammon and Moab and Mount Seir who were invading Judah, and they were defeated"* (2 Chronicles 20:21–22 NIV).

Notice the timing: **as they began to sing and praise.** The victory didn't happen after the battle ended. The breakthrough came the moment worship rose up.

When you choose worship instead of fear, complaining, or panic, you shift the atmosphere of the battle. You invite God's presence to fight for you. Worship in warfare is an act of faith. It is declaring God's greatness when the situation looks hopeless, when the enemy is advancing, and when victory is still unseen.

Why Worship Works

1. **Worship Confuses the Enemy.**

   The enemy cannot comprehend faith-filled praise in the middle of adversity. When you sing in the fire, when you shout before the walls fall, when you dance in the face of disappointment—it disarms and disorients the kingdom of darkness. Your worship becomes a prophetic declaration of victory.

2. **Worship Centers Your Heart.**

   Fear magnifies the problem; worship magnifies God. Praise shifts your focus from the size of the battle to the greatness of the One who already won. Worship re-centers your heart in truth: *"The battle is not mine—it belongs to the Lord"* (2 Chronicles 20:15).

3. **Worship Invites God's Strategy.**

   Throughout Scripture, victories often began with worship. At Jericho, the walls fell when the people shouted in obedience to God's command (Joshua 6). In Acts 16, Paul and Silas sang hymns in prison, and God shook the ground, broke their chains, and opened doors (Acts 16:25–26). Worship releases heaven's strategy on earth

Worship in Your Battle

The question is not *if* you will face battles—it is *how* you will face them. Will you panic, complain, and be fearful? Or will you worship your way into victory?

- When fear rises, lift your hands in worship – **Yadah.**

- When discouragement comes, shout in worship! – **Shabach**.
- When you feel unworthy, bow in worship and remember His grace and His mercy – **Barak**
- When chains try to bind you, sing in worship – **Zamar**

Worship is not emotional hype. It is *prophetic action*. It is aligning with God when everything around you looks like defeat.

Reflection Questions

1. Where in your life do you need to respond with worship instead of worry?
2. How has complaining or fear affected your ability to hear God's strategy?
3. Which type of praise (Towdah, Yadah, Barak, Shabach, Zamar, Halal, Tehillah) do you need to incorporate more intentionally?

Prayer Focus

1. **Worship as Warfare**

   Father, I choose to worship You in the middle of my battles. Let my praise shift my mindset from fear to faith. Let my worship confuse the enemy and release your strategies for victory. Train me to worship until I see the victory.

Key Takeaway: Worship is not just preparation for war—it is war. Praise shifts atmospheres, confuses the enemy, and invites God's power to bring victory.

CHAPTER 18

Spiritual Boldness

(WEEK 3 - DAY 18)

The Call to Boldness

Today I want to remind you of a truth many believers overlook: *intimacy with God produces boldness.*

Proverbs 28:1 declares: *"The wicked flee though no one pursues, but the righteous are as bold as a lion."* This boldness is not arrogance or recklessness. It is confidence rooted in knowing who you are in Christ and what authority you carry as His child.

True boldness flows from relationship. The more time you spend in His presence, the more fearless you become. You are not emboldened by your own strength but by the awareness that the Spirit of the Living God dwells in you.

The early church understood this. After facing threats from religious leaders, they did not pray for safety or protection. Instead, they prayed: *"Now, Lord, consider their threats and enable your servants to speak your word with great boldness"* (Acts 4:29). The result? Scripture says the place where they prayed was shaken, they were filled with the Holy Spirit, and they spoke the Word of God boldly (Acts 4:31).

When God's Spirit fills you, *fear gives way to courage, hesitation turns to obedience, and your life becomes a living testimony of His power.*

Breaking Fear and Intimidation

Fear and intimidation are some of the enemy's most effective weapons. If left unchecked, they will silence your voice, paralyze your steps, and keep you from stepping into the fullness of all that God has for you.

Think about it: how many opportunities to witness, to serve, or to obey have been lost because of fear? Fear whispers: *"What will people think?"* Intimidation arises: *"You're not ready. You're not qualified."*

But God's Word answers clearly: *"For God has not given us a spirit of fear, but of power and of love and of a sound mind"* (2 Timothy 1:7).

To walk in boldness, you must reject fear and confront intimidation with truth.

Walking in boldness requires three key commitments:

1. **Knowing your identity in Christ.** You are not ordinary—you are chosen, seated with Christ in heavenly places, and clothed with His authority (Ephesians 2:6).
2. **Trusting the Holy Spirit's empowerment.** Boldness is not natural; it is supernatural. It is the Spirit of God working through you (Acts 1:8).
3. **Choosing obedience over comfort.** Boldness is not the absence of fear—it is the decision to obey God in spite of it.

The moment you choose obedience, heaven backs you up.

Living Boldly in Your Assignment

Boldness is not just for apostles, pastors, or prophets. Every believer is called to boldness because every believer is called to witness.

- Boldness looks like speaking truth with love when silence feels safer.
- Boldness looks like stepping into your God-given assignment even when you feel inadequate.
- Boldness looks like sharing the gospel with a friend or coworker, even if rejection is possible.
- Boldness looks like standing firm in righteousness, even when culture pushes compromise.

Daniel boldly refused to bow to Babylon's idols. Esther boldly approached the king to intercede for her people. Peter boldly preached on Pentecost, and thousands were saved. Their boldness was not rooted in their personality – it was rooted in intimacy and obedience to God.

The same Spirit who emboldened them lives in you.

Reflection Questions

1. In what areas of your life do you struggle with fear or intimidation?
2. What would it look like for you to step into boldness in those specific areas this week?
3. How can you daily remind yourself of your identity and authority in Christ?
4. What's one act of obedience you've been delaying because of fear?

Prayer Focus

1. **Boldness and Courage**

   Father, fill me with holy boldness through Your Spirit. Break the grip of fear and hesitation in my life. Teach me to walk in confidence, not confidence in myself but in Christ who lives in me. Empower me to speak truth with love, to obey without delay, and to be a witness of Your power wherever I go. Let my life reflect the boldness of a lion because I belong to the Lion of Judah.

Key Takeaway: Boldness comes from intimacy with God and knowing your authority in Christ. Walk boldly—you are not alone.

CHAPTER 19

You Are Meant to Shine

[WEEK 3 - DAY 19]

Shining in Darkness

From the very beginning, God designed you to shine. Not to draw attention to yourself, but to reflect His glory into a world desperate for hope.

Jesus said, *"You are the light of the world. A city set on a hill cannot be hidden"* (Matthew 5:14). Being a carrier of light and shinning is not optional—it is your identity in Christ. Just as the moon reflects the sun, you were created to reflect the Son of God—His love, His truth, His character—into every environment you step into.

Light doesn't have to announce itself. Its presence speaks for itself. Darkness flees when light appears. That means every time you step into a room filled with darkness – tension, confusion, despair, or heaviness – you have the ability to shift the atmosphere simply by walking in who God called you to be. Somebody born blind and has lived in darkness all their lives will not know they are in darkness until they experience the appearance of light. Your very presence should expose darkness and dispel it.

Shining is not about being perfect, loud, or flashy. It's about living in such a way that people see Christ through your words, actions, and attitude. It's about bringing clarity where there is confusion, hope where there is despair, and joy where there is heaviness. Your light points others to the Source—Jesus Himself.

What Keeps Us From Shining?

If Light is our identity, why do so many believers live hidden, dimmed, or ineffective lives? Jesus addresses this in Matthew 5:15: *"Neither do people light a lamp and put it under a bowl. Instead, they put it on its stand, and it gives light to everyone in the house."*

The truth is, many of us cover our light. We allow fear, insecurity, or compromise to dim what God designed to shine.

Common "bowls" that keep believers from shining:

1. **Fear** – Fear of rejection, criticism, or standing out can silence your witness. But God has not given you a spirit of fear (2 Timothy 1:7).
2. **Insecurity** – Believing the lie that you are unqualified, too broken, or too weak keeps you from stepping out. But your light is not about your perfection – it's about Christ's perfection and He lives in you!
3. **Compromise** – When we blend in with culture instead of living set apart, our light is dimmed. Light cannot serve its purpose if it dimmed and cannot dispel the darkness.
4. **Distraction** – Being too busy or preoccupied can cause you to miss moments where God is calling you to step into a situation and reflect Him, reflect His light. You miss opportunities to shine.

Jesus calls us to come out of obscurity and let our light shine brightly. This will mean:

- *Living authentically* – Living as Christ has instructed us to live because our identity is in Him. Choosing integrity when it is easier to blend in.
- *Serving others* – Meeting needs quietly, without expecting recognition and by doing so transforming lives and bringing glory to His name.
- *Carrying joy and hope* – Allowing the presence of God in you to shift the atmosphere wherever you go. You are a change agent because you are the extension of His hands and feet on earth.

Called to Influence

You were never meant to live a dim or hidden life. You were created to influence. Light naturally impacts everything around it – it doesn't struggle to shine. It shines because that is its nature!

Philippians 2:15 says you are to *"shine among them like stars in the sky."* Stars don't compete with darkness—they stand out because they dispel the darkness! Likewise, God has placed you exactly where you are—your family, workplace, school, or community—so that your life will stand out and point others to Him.

Isaiah 60:1 declares: *"Arise, shine, for your light has come, and the glory of the Lord rises upon you."* The command is not "create" light, but "arise" and allow what God has placed within you to come forth and shine. *God's glory is in you – now it is time to reflect it.*

Reflection Questions

1. What "bowl" has kept your light hidden?
2. Where has God placed you to be a light that cannot be hidden?
3. What would it look like to practically let your light shine today in one small but intentional way?
4. How might your influence change if you lived every day aware that you are a city on a hill that cannot be hidden?

Prayer Focus

1. **Shine Brightly**

    Father, thank You for making me light in a dark world. Remove fear, insecurity, distraction, or compromise that dims my light. Fill me with boldness, joy, and courage so I can shine brightly for You wherever I go. Use my words, actions, and presence to point others to Jesus. Let my life glorify You in both big and small ways.

Key Takeaway: You were made to shine—not in your strength, but as a reflection of Christ in you. When you let your light shine, others are drawn to Him.

CHAPTER 20

Declare the Victory

(WEEK 3 - DAY 20)

The Power of Declaration

Victory is our portion because we are in Christ. He already given us the victory over sin, death, and the grave by nailing them to the cross. (1 Corinthians 15:57)

Words carry power. Proverbs 18:21 reminds us: *"The tongue has the power of life and death, and those who love it will eat its fruit."* What you declare determines what you see in your life.

Declarations are not empty slogans or wishful thinking. They are *faith-filled proclamations rooted in God's Word.* When you declare His Truth, those words have the power to go forth and bring to pass the things they were sent to accomplish. You are shifting the spiritual and physical realms into agreement with what God has already spoken.

When the walls of Jericho came crashing down, it wasn't military strength that secured the victory, it was obedience to God's unusual instructions. After marching around the city, Joshua commanded the people to shout before the walls came down (Joshua 6:16, 20). It was the declaration of victory before the breakthrough that released the power of God because God had already ordained the victory for His people!

In the same way, many battles in your life will only shift when you *open your mouth and declare what God has already spoken concerning that battle.*

Why Declare the Victory?

Faith Speaks Before It Sees.

Hebrews 11:1 defines faith as confidence in what we hope for and assurance about what we do not yet see. Romans 4:17 says God *"calls into being things that were not."* When you declare victory, you are exercising faith by speaking into existence that which is yet unseen. Declarations align your life with what God has already promised.

Declarations Shift Atmospheres.

When you speak God's promises aloud, you are not only reminding yourself – you are reminding and shifting the environment around you to comply. Declarations combat negativity, silence lies, and fill the atmosphere with Truth. David did this when he declared, *"This day the Lord will deliver you into my hands"* (1 Samuel 17:46), before Goliath ever fell.

Declarations Agree with Heaven.

Jesus taught us to pray, *"Your kingdom come, Your will be done, on earth as it is in heaven"* (Matthew 6:10). Every time you declare God's Word, you are partnering with heaven to bring His will into your situation. It is a way of saying: *"Lord, let my life reflect what You have already decreed in heaven."*

Breaking Negative Declarations

Just as positive declarations release life, negative ones can bring chaos, confusion, stagnation, even death and destruction. Words of doubt, fear, or hopelessness give the enemy an open door. Many times, believers sabotage their own progress with phrases like: *"I'll never change." "This always happens to me." "Things will never get better." "Maybe I wasn't meant to .... (be free, be healed, have joy, have peace etc)."*

But you don't have to live under the weight of negative words. You can cancel them in the name of Jesus and replace them with declarations of Truth.

Instead of *"I'll never change"* → declare *"Old things have passed away and I am a new creation in Christ."* (2 Corinthians 5:17). *"I have the mind of Christ. He is providing the requisite knowledge and wisdom that I need to change."* (1Corinthians 2:16)

Instead of *"This will destroy me"* → declare *"No weapon formed against me shall prosper"* (Isaiah 54:17).

Instead of *"I can't do this"* → declare *"I can do all things through Christ who strengthens me"* (Philippians 4:13).

Every time you replace a lie with Truth and declare it, you are tearing down a stronghold and releasing faith.

How to Declare the Victory

Declarations are powerful, but they must be intentional. Here are steps to help you practice daily declarations:

1. **Find the Word.** Identify the promise in Scripture that speaks to your situation.

2. **Write it Down.** Turn that scripture into a declaration. Example: Philippians 4:19 → *"My God supplies all my needs according to His riches in glory."*
3. **Speak it Aloud.** Don't just think it—say it. Let your ears hear your own mouth agree with God.
4. **Repeat Daily.** Declarations build faith through repetition. Just as negative self-talk can shape your mindset, faith declarations renew your mind.
5. **Take Action.** Ask God to give you steps that you can take in faith. Then obey! Think of Joshua and the wall of Jericho,
6. **Mix with Worship.** Pair your declarations with praise. Declare victory, then worship as if it's already done.

Reflection Questions

1. What negative words have you spoken about yourself, your family, or your future that you need to cancel?
2. What promises of God do you need to declare today?
3. How would your perspective shift if you consistently declared victory over fear, doubt, and obstacles?
4. What "Jericho wall" in your life needs to hear your shout of victory today?

Prayer Focus

1. **Victory and Authority**

   Father, thank You for giving me victory through Jesus Christ. I repent for every negative word I've spoken over myself or my situation. Today, I cancel their power in the name of Jesus. I choose to declare Your Word over my life. I declare that I am more than a conqueror, that no weapon formed against me will prosper, and that every promise You have made is yes and amen in Christ. Train me to use my words as weapons of victory, and let my declarations align with your Truth.

Key Takeaway: Victory is already yours in Christ. Declare it boldly, stand on His promises, and watch walls fall and situations shift.

CHAPTER 21

A New Beginning

(WEEK 3 - DAY 21)

The Journey Continues

Congratulations! You have completed the 21-Day Intimacy Challenge. That is no small accomplishment. You've shown up daily, pressed past distractions, wrestled through resistance, and chosen to make space for God. God has taken notice.

But hear this clearly: **today is not an ending—it is a beginning.**

God never designed intimacy with Him to be a seasonal pursuit or a temporary discipline. His invitation is not limited to 21 days— it is a lifelong call into daily communion, ongoing surrender, and continual transformation.

Over the past three weeks, you have learned to still your heart before God, to hunger for His presence, to surrender your will, to intercede, to use worship as a weapon, and to declare victory by faith. You have broken patterns, silenced lies, and embraced your identity in Christ.

These are not one-time actions. They are lifelong strategies. They are the foundations of a lifestyle of intimacy with God. The goal of these

21 days was never to "check a box," but to equip you with habits that will carry you into your next season—and the one after that.

Why Today Matters

Intimacy Uncovers Purpose.

When you are intimate with God and your life is rooted in Him, your purpose becomes clear. You don't have to strive to figure out who you are or what you're called to do—identity flows out of intimacy. As you remain in Him, you bear fruit that lasts (John 15:5).

Consistency Builds Power.

Growth is never found in what we do occasionally – it is achieved through consistency. Word study, Prayer, fasting, and worship may seem small in the moment, yet over time they shape your character, renew your mind, and transform your destiny. Small disciplines, practiced with faithfulness, produce great power. And true power doesn't rise from comfort—it's forged in fire, in discipline, in trials, and in the will to come out stronger.

You Are a Kingdom Ambassador.

What you've gained is not just for you. God has called you to shine in the world, to be salt and light, to influence others by living as an ambassador of His Kingdom. Your intimacy with Him becomes a witness to those around you. *Your transformation makes way for someone else's breakthrough.*

Stepping Into the Next Season

This challenge was a launching pad, not a finish line. God is calling you to:

- *Keep the fire burning.* Don't let your hunger for Him fade. Keep setting aside time for prayer, fasting, and the Word. Time in silence to listen to Him.
- *Guard your intimacy.* Distractions will try to creep back in. Be intentional about protecting the secret place.
- *Multiply what you've learned.* Share your journey. Disciple others. Invite friends, family, or your community to walk in intimacy with God too.
- *Live with expectancy.* The same God who met you during these 21 days will continue to reveal Himself in greater ways if you remain hungry and surrendered.

Reflection Questions

1. What has changed in your relationship with God during these 21 days?
2. Which new habits or disciplines will you carry forward into the next season?
3. Who is God calling you to influence, encourage, or disciple with what you've learned?
4. What vision is God giving you for your next season?

Prayer Focus

1. **A Lifestyle of Intimacy**

   Father, thank You for drawing me close during these 21 days. Thank You for every moment of revelation, correction, encouragement, and breakthrough. I dedicate myself to walking with You daily—not just for a season, but for a lifetime. Strengthen me to remain consistent in prayer, worship, fasting, and Your Word. Guard my heart from distraction. Let my life shine as a reflection of Your love and power, and use me to draw others closer to You. This is only the beginning. Take me deeper, Lord.

Key Takeaway: This is only the beginning. Keep pursuing intimacy with God daily, and watch Him transform every area of your life.

CONTINUE THE JOURNEY

Your 21 days are just the beginning.

God's heart for you is intimacy – not just for a season but for a lifetime.

If this devotional has stirred your hunger for Him, we invite you to take the next step:

- *Testify* – We would love to hear how God has blessed you by this teaching. Send testimonies to: support@ newcovenantministry.org
- *Join our 21-Day Intimacy Fast* – Experience live teaching, prayer calls, and a supportive global community pursuing God together.
- *Connect with Us* – Stay updated on upcoming challenges, teachings, and resources to help you grow.

Scan the QR code to join the community and be part of what God is doing.

(If you're outside the fast dates, you can still sign up to receive updates and bonus resources to deepen your intimacy with Him year-round.)

Your heart has encountered His—don't stop here. Continue to pursue Him, and watch what He will do.

LET'S STAY CONNECTED

Follow us on social media for weekly encouragement, teaching, prayer updates, and community. Share what God is doing in your life using the hashtag **#21DIntimacyChallenge** – we'd love to celebrate with you!

- Instagram: [@newcovenantministries_]
- Instagram: [@abioyebode]
- Instagram: [@livegrowthrive_]
- Facebook: [https://www.facebook.com/groups/ 1980519719348889/]
- Website: [www.newcovenantministry.org]

ABOUT THE AUTHOR

Abi Oyebode is the founder and leader of the annual 21-Day Intimacy Challenge Fast, a global movement inspiring believers to pursue God with intention, passion, and expectation. Known for her prophetic insight, relatable teaching style, and compassionate heart, she has helped countless people break through spiritual barriers, deepen their relationship with God, and live boldly in their God-given purpose.

www.ingramcontent.com/pod-product-compliance
Lightning Source LLC
LaVergne TN
LVHW051422080426
835508LV00022B/3201